The 28 Day Plan

CELLULITE BUSTER

Christine Green

p

This is a Parragon Book

First published by Parragon 2002

Parragon
Queen Street House
4 Queen Street
Bath BA1 1HE, UK

Designed, produced and packaged by
Stonecastle Graphics Limited

Text by Christine Green
Edited by Gillian Haslam
Designed by Sue Pressley and Paul Turner
Commissioned photography by Roddy Paine

ISBN 0-75256-793-4

Printed in China

Disclaimer

The exercises and advice detailed in this book
assume that you are a normally healthy adult.
Therefore the author, publishers, their servants or
agents cannot accept responsibility for loss or
damage suffered by individuals as a result of
following advice or attempting an exercise or
treatment referred to in this book. It is strongly
recommended that individuals intending to
undertake an exercise programme and any
change of diet do so following consultation with
their doctor.

Contents

Cellulite

Do you suffer with cellulite? Those areas of puckered, dimpling skin on the upper part of the thighs or buttocks which, no matter what you have done, refuse to budge? Don't worry – eight out of ten women are affected with this unsightly problem, even the rich and famous who always look so perfectly groomed.

Sadly there are no 7-day wonder creams that can make it vanish or miracle cures that can eliminate it, unless you have the finances to pay for Ionithermie or Caci treatments at beauty salons. However, the good news is that with time, effort and determination you can do something about it yourself and if you follow this 28-day programme, you will end up with the smoothest, sexiest legs on the beach this summer!

What is cellulite?

To understand what you are dealing with it is important to know what cellulite is and how it is formed. Firstly, cellulite is not fat.

Although there are varying theories from different experts, the one fundamental point upon which they all agree is that it must be assumed it is a hormonal factor, because the condition largely affects women. And the guilty party has been pinpointed down to oestrogen – the more there is present in the body, the higher the probability of cellulite developing.

Before placing all the blame on oestrogen, remember that it does have an important role to play in preparing the female body to receive an embryo, and if there is an egg to fertilize the amount of oestrogen drops. Scientific studies have found that women in general now have far more oestrogen in their bodies than ever before. Unfortunately cellulite is created when there is an overload of oestrogen-causing waste matter being transported away from various organs.

Simultaneously, as this build up of oestrogen is pushing the waste away, we are eating foods that contain great amounts of preservatives, chemicals and additives which add to the excess waste already present in the body. The result is overload and sluggish circulation, and help is needed.

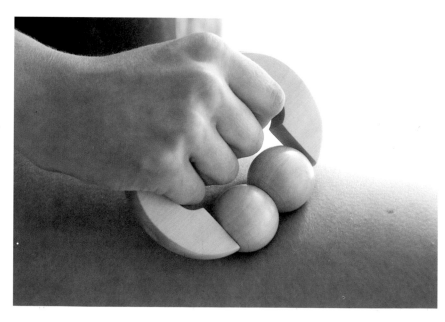

Cellulite – the facts
- Cellulite is not flab and it is not fat
- Over 95% of women have some cellulite on their bodies
- It very rarely appears in men
- In France, cellulite has been accepted as a genuine medical condition for the last 40 years
- It is not related to the size of the person – even top models get it

How to recognise cellulite

You will know you have cellulite by lightly pinching or pressing an area of tissue at the top of your thighs between your finger and thumb. Normal fat appears fairly smooth, but cellulite will reveal dimples, described as the skin of an orange. Strangely enough, cellulite tissue is also more sensitive and can often feel cold when touched and may appear whiter than other parts of your skin.

So now you know how it is formed and how to test whether you have it, you are likely to be more interested in discovering how to get rid of it. But first of all, there are other possible contributory factors to the formation of cellulite to be considered.

Bad diet: poor eating habits, too much caffeine or alcohol, and spicy foods can all cause the formation of cellulite because the toxins they produce get trapped in the fatty tissue.

Smoking: bad news all round, not only for the skin and lungs but for the damage it brings to the connective tissue that causes the dimpling effect of cellulite.

Lack of water: water is the body's best friend, especially those with cellulite. As well as re-hydrating the body, it helps flush out toxins and accumulated waste from the system. It is important to drink at least 6-8 glasses each day, more if you can.

Lifestyle: those who are employed in office jobs and spend all day sitting at a desk are more prone to the development of cellulite due to an overall sluggish circulation, especially in the buttocks and thigh areas. Try to get up every hour or so and have a walk around, even if it is just a visit to the loo. And at lunchtime, make sure you go out for a walk.

Lack of exercise: exercise is the best thing you can do for your body. It improves muscle tone, circulation and overall well being, helping to break up blocked tissue and purify the blood.

How to get rid of cellulite

In order to deal with cellulite it helps to understand a little of our fat anatomy. Beneath the surface of the skin there is a thin layer of subcutaneous fat whose role is to cushion the body against a sudden trauma. It also keeps the body warm. Delve deeper and there is another layer of fat called the scarpus fascia that controls the bumps and various bulges in our body. This is the dreaded area where fat cells lurk and which enlarge as we gain weight. But it is also subdivided into chambers via connective tissue which holds the top layer of skin to those layers underneath. Once the connective tissue weakens and misshapes, it pulls on the surface of the skin and thus creates the dimpled effect on the skin called cellulite.

How to help yourself

We've already mentioned there are lots of costly treatments and various creams that are purported to eradicate cellulite from the body but the problem is, they can be expensive and, furthermore, do they actually work?

Why spend money when you can have the knowledge at your fingertips and by following a combination of diet, dry skin brushing, massage and the use of certain essential oils you can deal very effectively with cellulite yourself.

Diet: experts recommend people with cellulite follow a detoxifying diet that includes eating plenty of fresh fruits, vegetables and whole grains. Not only will it cleanse and detoxify the entire system, thus enabling

Remember, cellulite loves:

✗ Sitting around too much
✗ Processed and refined foods
✗ Coffee
✗ Alcohol
✗ Neglecting one's body
SO DON'T DO THEM!

Remember, cellulite hates:

✓ Exercise
✓ Low-fat diet
✓ Lots of water
✓ Regular beauty pampering
✓ Skin brushing
SO DO THEM!

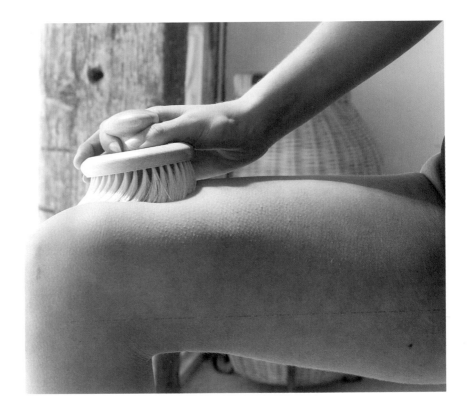

toxic wastes to be eradicated, but will prevent further cellulite forming.

Dry skin brushing: a highly effective method for stimulating the hard particles of matter in the lymphatic system, which hinder the elimination of the toxins from the system.

Aromatherapy: the therapeutic benefits of using essential oils in the treatment of eradicating cellulite have long been recognized.

Relaxation: stress and worry make cellulite worse by releasing extra adrenaline into the system and causing the liver to work overtime by eradicating the excess. Spend time relaxing and deep breathing, allowing your lungs to fill with oxygen and thus greatly improving the circulation.

Massage: if you go to a beauty salon for professional treatment of cellulite you will probably find they use a combination of aromatherapy and massage known as lymphatic drainage massage – a hard kneading of the skin which pummels and works away at the cellulite deposits at the same time as activating the lymph nodes. You can learn to do this at home (see Daily Treatments).

Things that can make cellulite worse:

• Tight clothing
• The contraceptive pill: experts believe the release of complex biochemical substances into the body can interfere with the body's metabolism and help cause the formation of cellulite
• Sunshine: the dimpling effect may be made worse by sunbathing since excessive exposure to the sunlight is known to cause the skin to lose its elasticity

Exercising Cellulite Away

Cellulite just loves the person who doesn't exercise, who'd far rather take the car to the
shops and whose one and only physical activity is to climb the stairs to bed!
This has got to change if you want to banish that cellulite.

Just take a look at female athletes and see how
toned and lean their legs are without a sign of
puckered skin. The reason is their active lifestyle
doesn't give cellulite a chance to settle, and you can
be like that too by including a disciplined exercise
routine into your programme.

Home exercises

Would you like your legs to look well toned with not
a glimmer of cellulite and be able to flaunt them off
at the beach in your brand new bathing costume?
Here is a selection of stretching and toning exercises
that will help you achieve that dream, and which can
be done in the comfort and privacy of your own home.

Remember, before you begin do some gentle
warming up exercises to flex and stretch the muscles
and thereby prevent any possible injury. Gentle
jogging on the spot followed by some stretching
exercises should suffice. And when the routine is
complete, do the same cooling down exercises to
return the heart rate to normal.

Plan to do three exercise sessions a week, each
lasting 30 minutes. But if this is too much, split the
routine into three 10-minute sessions spread
throughout the day.

It is all a matter of choice, just do what feels right
for your body and don't over exert yourself. Exercising
should be fun.

**Before starting any exercise programme you
should see your GP if you:**
- Have been inactive for some time
- Are a woman aged over 50
- Suffer heart or lung disease, high blood
  pressure, diabetes, arthritis or asthma
- Are a smoker
- Are overweight
- Are pregnant
- Are concerned in any way about your health

Hip and thigh exercises

Choose three of the following and repeat them
10 times daily:

Squat

A great exercise for the thighs and buttocks
1. Stand with feet hip-width apart, with the left foot
45-60cm (18-24in) behind the right one and slightly
bent at the knee.
2. Keep both arms by your sides. Keep back straight
and head up with chin parallel to the floor.
3. Slowly bend both legs and lower your body. Take it
easy and don't worry if you can't do it the first few
times. Just concentrate and do the movements in your
own time. Stop if you feel pressure on your knees.
4. Change sides to work the other leg.

Inner thigh toner

1. Lie on the floor on your side, with one arm
supporting your head.
2. With the lower leg bent and resting on the floor,
raise the top leg off the floor as far as you are able
without straining, hold and then gently lower it back
to the floor.
3. Once you have done one side, turn over and work
on the other leg.

Bottom toner

1. Lie on your front, hands resting on top of one
another, chin resting lightly on top.
2. Raise one leg about 12.5cm (5in) off the floor and
hold for a count of 10.
3. Slowly lower the leg back to the floor and repeat
with the other leg.

Hip toner 1

1. Stand sideways with your hand resting on a chair, knees slightly bent, shoulders relaxed.
2. Slowly raise your right leg, making sure you keep both your body and raised foot facing forwards.
3. Carefully and slowly lower your leg.
4. Turn around and repeat with the other leg.

Hip toner 2

1. Stand facing the back of a chair. With both hands resting on the chair, stand with knees slightly bent, shoulders relaxed.
2. Slowly raise your right leg out to the side, making sure you keep both your body and raised foot facing forwards.
3. Carefully and slowly lower your leg.
4. Repeat with the other leg.

Lunges

These are ideal for working on the thighs and buttocks and perfect for doing at home. If you feel you need weights, grab hold of a couple of cans of beans.

1. Place hands on hips and stand up straight. Alternatively, hold a weight in each hand and stand up straight with palms facing in towards your body.
2. Place your feet hip width apart. Keep head up with chin parallel to the ground.
3. Take one step forward, slowly bending both knees so the front knee aligns with the ankle and the rear heel is lifted.
4. Don't allow your back knee to touch the floor.
5. Push yourself back up. Stop if pain occurs in knee joints or ligaments.
6. Alternate this action on the other leg.

Housework and related duties can burn up various amounts of calories:
- Climbing the stairs burns up 10 calories a minute
- Vacuuming can burn up 6 calories a minute
- One hour's worth of digging in the garden can burn up 392 calories

Upper arms

If you find that you have traces of cellulite on the backs of upper arms, try this exercise.

1. Fill a 3-litre (5-pint) empty plastic pop bottle with water to use as a weight.
2. Sit on a seat.
3. Take the bottle in one hand and move it over your head, palm facing inwards.
4. Slowly bend your elbow so that you are bringing the bottle down to your shoulder but without altering the upper arm position.
5. Lift the arm up and repeat the same process again.
6. Do this exercise six times with one arm and six with the other.

Stomach exercises

It is worthwhile doing a few pelvic lifts before you to any stomach exercises. Pelvic lifts help to strengthen and protect the muscles that run under your pelvis from your pubic bone through to your bottom.

Pelvic lift

You can do this standing, with legs parallel, hip-width apart, or lying on your back on the floor with knees raised, feet flat on the floor hip-width apart. Contract the muscles that you would use to stop the flow of urine, hold for five seconds then relax and repeat five times.

This is an exercise which can be performed standing almost anywhere at any time.

Tummy crunchers

1. Lie on your back with your knees bent and your feet flat on the floor, hip-width apart.
2. Tilt your pelvis until your lower back is pressed flat against the floor.
3. Rest your hands lightly against the side of your head.
4. Now slowly lift your head and shoulders a little way off the floor.
5. Hold for a few seconds and then lower back down to the floor.
6. Repeat 15–20 times.

Exercising outside

Sometimes exercising in the house can get a little boring, so why not go outside for a change or combine your exercise programme with some outdoor activities?

If you find choosing an appropriate exercise a little difficult, the best ones for dealing with cellulite are those that will help firm and tone up the legs, hips and bottom. Ideally aim to work out for between 20-40 minutes each time and as your stamina increases, then you can build on to the time.

Cycling: the ideal exercise for firming the fronts and backs of your thighs.

Tennis: there is no better exercise than tennis for promoting shapely legs.

Power walking: according to experts you don't have to work up a sweat at the gym on a workout to tone up your muscles – a brisk walk is just as good. In fact the medical profession agrees that the health benefits associated with walking exceed those of every other form of exercise.

Power walking can:
- help you shape up and at the same time burn approximately 350 calories an hour
- lower cholesterol
- regulate blood pressure
- relieve chronic pain
- help insomnia and infertility
- alleviate depression

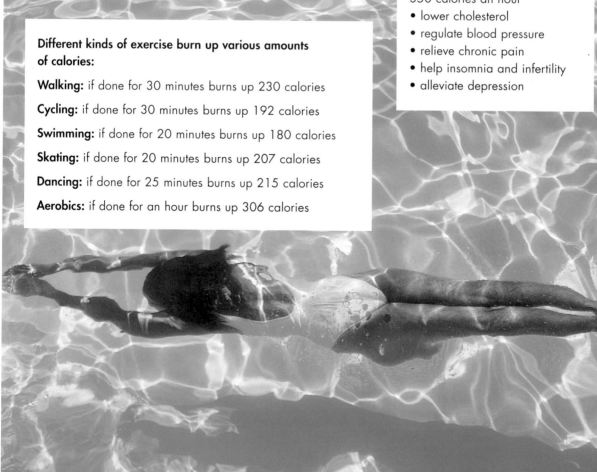

Different kinds of exercise burn up various amounts of calories:

Walking: if done for 30 minutes burns up 230 calories

Cycling: if done for 30 minutes burns up 192 calories

Swimming: if done for 20 minutes burns up 180 calories

Skating: if done for 20 minutes burns up 207 calories

Dancing: if done for 25 minutes burns up 215 calories

Aerobics: if done for an hour burns up 306 calories

What better all-round form of exercise could you ask for? To get the full benefit, aim to do three or four 20-minute sessions of brisk walking a week. The technique is simple: shoulders back, neck relaxed, shoulders aligned directly above your hips and a heel-toe roll in a straight line through the foot narrowing the width of your track to allow for greater speed with arms and legs moving in sync. Each week try to improve on your last efforts by going a little further. Always warm up and cool down before and afterwards.

Aerobics: no better exercise for strengthening and toning the legs as well as the rest of the body. Join in a local gym.

Step classes: these help to sculpt the legs but make sure you don't do more than one class a week otherwise you will risk bulking up your legs too much.

Spinning: one of the latest fitness crazes. The classes entail riding really quickly on a special exercise bike while the instructor keeps you pedalling with different techniques and music. A 45-minute workout can apparently burn up an amazing 500 calories. Your local gym may well have more details.

Water: if you exercise in water, it is 15 times more effective than doing that same exercise on land simply because of the resistance against your muscles. Water is a superb and quick way to tone your body because whichever direction you move, your body will still have to push against the water.

Skipping: indoors or outdoors, skipping is the ideal all-over workout and perfect for stretching the leg muscles. It also works the heart, lungs and upper body to get a really good workout. You may have to start in bursts of 2-3 minutes but you will be pleasantly surprised how quickly the body adapts.

Spare minute exercises

Here are two simple exercises that can be done in any spare moment – whilst washing the dishes, waiting in the bus queue, even when serving dinner!

Bum clencher Clench your buttocks, hold for a few seconds and then simply release – perfect for toning up the buttocks.

Thigh firmer When waiting for the kettle to boil, gradually raise and lower your leg straight behind and as high as you can, almost like a ballerina. Hold the position for 30 seconds and then repeat with the other leg.

Helpful Treatments

There are lots of other treatments that can help deal with banishing cellulite and will therefore prove invaluable included in the programme, each of which have their own benefits.

Your daily routine every day until the third week should be skin brushing, aromatherapy, and massage. After the third week use the massage oils every alternate day.

Dry skin brushing

Skin brushing is one of the most effective and cheapest ways of encouraging the drainage of excess fluid from those areas of the body prone to cellulite. In order for it to be truly effective and enable the lymphatic system to clear itself and expel waste, it must be done on a daily basis, often for several months, and applied with a special brush with hard and scratchy bristles. Five minutes of dry skin brushing per day can:

- improve digestion
- aid metabolism
- impart new levels of energy
- dissipate cellulite

How to do it

Give yourself an overall body brush and feel the overall benefits. Begin by brushing your fingers and hands. Hold your fingers outstretched and brush in between them several times before moving on to the hand, and then the palms before doing the other hand.

Using long strokes, take the brush from the wrist to the elbow and then from the elbow to the shoulder. Remember to use long, firm, bold strokes and always brush towards the heart to encourage the blood flow.

Feet and toes are next. Resting one leg on the side of the bath or a chair, sweep across the toes and then the soles of the feet, moving around the leg and up from the ankle. This should be done approximately 14 times.

The thighs and buttocks are next. When you brush the thighs work upwards, as vigorously as you can, concentrating on the areas where cellulite is particularly evident. Finally, brush the buttocks firmly in any direction. Generally, skin brushing should be performed in the direction of the heart, but circular movements around the buttocks are best. After working on the lower body, graduate up to the neck and brush downwards from the head to the shoulders.

The front and sides of the body are next. Don't brush over the nipples but gently applying pressure around the breasts is fine. Don't brush the stomach and abdomen but move on to the back, using long firm strokes.

Don't expect miracles overnight – you will probably need to do this at least every other day to be most effective, although some people do it every day. Never brush over broken skin. If the skin is red and scratched after brushing, the next day take it a little more gently.

Aromatherapy

For many people aromatherapy oil means something they add to their bathwater as an aid to relaxation. There are hundreds of different essential oils, each with their own inherent properties and you can easily learn how to use some of them in your programme.

There are various special anti-cellulite oils on the market, based on the principles of aromatherapy, which are a combination of essential oils diluted in correct carrier oils and you are advised to buy them from a health shop where you can ask advice. Remember to check if your chosen oil is suitable for application to the skin once diluted in carrier oil. This is especially important if you are pregnant.

How to use essential oils

After body brushing, shake three or four drops of essential oil into the bathwater and soak for about 20 minutes. During this time take in deep breaths. As you lie in the bath knead and pummel the cellulite areas.

Once out of the bath and dry, massage some diluted oil into each thigh and the buttocks, paying particular attention to those cellulite areas. You may also wish to rub some diluted oil over your stomach and so increase detoxification. This treatment is best performed either first thing in the morning or early evening.

Yoga

It may sound rather odd thinking that yoga can help deal with cellulite, but those who practise yoga fervently very rarely suffer with it. It seems that all the stretching and flexing of muscles activates the circulation of blood and other fluids around the body.

It may be a good idea to see if there are any local yoga classes to join or why not visit the library to borrow some yoga books and a video to do at home.

Essential oils said to be effective anti-cellulite oils:

- Black pepper
- Geranium
- Patchouli
- Clary sage
- Juniper
- Rosemary
- Cypress
- Lemon
- Sandalwood

Self massage

In any successful cellulite programme massage is an important element. Daily massage will help you learn to identify those areas where cellulite has formed and you will also come to know your body in a different way. At the beginning do it every single day by body brushing first and then follow with a massage.

Massage is fundamental in dealing with the reduction of cellulite as it:

✓ encourages circulation and can stimulate blood flow
✓ improves digestion
✓ increases kidney function
✓ flushes out the lymphatic system by the elimination of toxins and waste

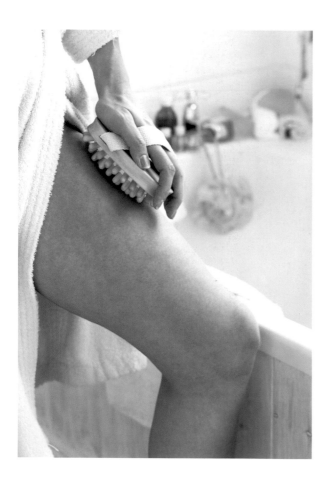

How to do it

Select an appropriate essential oil and pour a small amount into the palm of your hand and, using long stroking movements, begin at the ankle and work up to the knee and thigh using both hands, massaging the oil in well and making sure the movements are gentle but firm.

Experts recommend the best type of massage when dealing with cellulite is kneading, adopting the same action as though you were kneading dough. As you pick up the flesh you squeeze it, applying as much pressure as possible, almost as if you were punching areas of flesh.

Rolling is another useful movement for cellulite sufferers. This is where you pick up about an inch of flesh on the thigh and roll the flesh to break down the deposits.

After a time you will be able to identify those areas that contain more cellulite as they feel hard and grainy and as you apply pressure you will experience a ripple sensation.

Kneading and pinching at the flesh is something that you can do anytime and anywhere – when you are sitting watching television or waiting for the kettle to boil.

Detox bath

An Epsom salts bath is cheaper than many of the shop-bought preparations which contain seaweed and sea extracts which help eliminate toxins and fluid retention. Simply add 225–450g (^{1}/2–1lb) of Epsom salts to a hot bath and soak in it for 15 minutes.

Wrap up well afterwards and drink plenty of water as you will continue sweating and eliminating toxins for an hour or two. Try to rest for an hour after bathing.

Warning: Do not do this if you are pregnant or have heart problems.

Body scrubs

In order to improve the skin's texture and tone it up, body scrubs are worth including in the programme and should ideally be undertaken either before or during a shower, as they can be rather messy.

Scrubs involve massaging the skin with a gritty substance to remove dead skin cells and engrained grime and improve the overall appearance of the skin. They can either be used on their own or with a rough flannel or loofah to increase their effectiveness.

Body scrub recipe

50g (2oz) crunchy peanut butter
25g (1oz) finely ground sea salt
30ml (2 tablespoons) almond oil

Mix the peanut butter and sea salt together and stir in the almond oil to form a soft paste. Rub on to damp skin all over the body, paying greater attention to hard areas on the elbows, upper arms and knees. Rinse off with warm water, then have a shower.

Healthy Eating Plan

Dealing with cellulite isn't just about exercise. It is also about adopting a healthy eating plan, knowing which foods are better than others and eradicating those bad foods from your diet.

Unfortunately today's modern diet is a minefield for the cellulite sufferer due to its high sugar and fat content and with greater emphasis on processed and refined foods as opposed to fresh, natural ingredients. In truth, the body is a garbage bin to so much junk and rubbish that our liver, kidneys and bowels often find dealing with it too much. Once they have reached their capacity for elimination, the only alternative is for the waste to remain in the system.

Changing eating habits does not mean following a diet or calorie-counting, but it does mean watching that you eat healthy, nourishing food with a balance of essential nutrients derived from the following:

- Carbohydrates
- Proteins
- Fat
- Vitamins
- Minerals

Carbohydrates: these provide energy for the body and come in two types: simple carbohydrates which include basically sugar and very little else, and complex carbohydrates which include starchy foods such as bread, potatoes, cereal, pasta, rice, etc.

Protein: the body breaks down the protein from food into its component building blocks called amino acids that it then uses to build and repair tissue and muscle. Found in foods such as meat, poultry, fish, dairy foods such as cheese and yogurt, eggs, beans, lentils and nuts, cereals, etc.

Fat: number one enemy for the body but essential for helping to insulate and protect the organs and nerves. It is found in varying quantities in numerous foods such as butter, cheese, lard, dripping, snack foods, fatty meat, etc. The basic aim of a healthy diet is to reduce the amount of fat you eat and stick to a low-fat diet; it doesn't mean cutting them out totally, simply choosing those foods sensibly and checking on the label for low fat.

A healthy eating programme

The major part of a healthy eating programme consists of fresh fruit and vegetables, largely because of their abundance of minerals and vitamins. Canned and processed foods are best avoided as they contain additives and preservatives, but if you do find yourself having to eat some then make sure the greater proportion of that meal is salad or lightly steamed vegetables.

High in calories, nuts are also high in fibre, nutrients and potassium so are the ideal source of essential unsaturated fatty acids. Best eaten raw, unsalted and fresh.

Just as nuts are high in nutrients, so too are pulses and seeds and once fully sprouted their nutrient content increases. Great for adding flavour and colour to foods.

Fish is the perfect food as it contains all the vital

proteins. But as with most food, it is healthier eaten fresh rather than frozen which will be depleted of many essential nutrients. Smoked fish is fine provided it has been treated naturally. Avoid eating fish in brine as it is too salty. If selecting canned fish, those in olive or vegetable oil are the best.

Good foods for banishing cellulite

Fruit
- Apples
- Apricots
- Bilberries
- Blackberries
- Blackcurrants
- Blueberries
- Cherries
- Cranberries
- Currants
- Damsons
- Dates
- Figs
- Gooseberries
- Grapefruit
- Grapes
- Greengages
- Guavas
- Kiwi fruit
- Lemons
- Limes
- Loganberries
- Lychees
- Mangoes
- Melons
- Mulberries
- Nectarines
- Passionfruit
- Paw-paw
- Peaches
- Pears

- Pineapple
- Plums
- Pomegranates
- Prunes
- Quinces
- Raisins
- Raspberries
- Redcurrants
- Rhubarb
- Strawberries
- Sultanas

Vegetables
- Artichokes
- Asparagus
- Aubergines
- Beans (broad, butter, haricot, mung, runner, French, red kidney)
- Beansprouts
- Beetroot
- Broccoli
- Brussels sprouts
- Cabbage, (red, savoy, spring, white, winter)
- Carrots
- Cauliflower
- Celeriac
- Celery

- Chicory
- Chinese leaf
- Courgettes
- Cucumber
- Fennel
- Kohlrabi
- Leeks
- Lettuce
- Marrow
- Okra
- Onion
- Parsnips
- Peas
- Peppers (bell, capsicum)
- Plantain
- Potatoes
- Pumpkin
- Radishes
- Spring greens
- Spring onions
- Squashes
- Swede
- Sweetcorn
- Sweet potatoes
- Turnips
- Watercress
- Yams

Nuts
- Almonds

- Brazils
- Cashews
- Chestnuts
- Hazelnuts
- Macadamia nuts
- Pecans
- Pine nuts
- Pistachios
- Walnuts

Seeds, pulses and herbs
- Alfalfa
- Basil
- Cardamom pods
- Cayenne pepper
- Chillies
- Coriander
- Chickpeas
- Dill
- Fennel
- Ginger
- Lemongrass
- Marjoram
- Parsley
- Pepper
- Pumpkin seeds
- Rosemary
- Sage
- Sesame seeds
- Sunflower seeds

- Tarragon
- Thyme

Fish
- Cod
- Crab
- Haddock
- Halibut
- Herring
- Lemon sole
- Lobster
- Mackerel
- Monkfish
- Pilchards
- Plaice
- Prawns
- Salmon
- Sardines
- Scampi
- Shrimps
- Skate
- Trout
- Tuna

Non-dairy foods
- Goat's cheese/ milk/yogurt
- Sheep's milk/ cheese/yogurt
- Rice milk
- Soya milk

Reduce certain foods

The main aim of the diet is to enable the body to detoxify itself by eliminating long-held waste. It is not intended to be a weight-reducing diet, nor is it specifically intended as a diet only suitable for those who have cellulite to lose. The key word in fighting cellulite is purification not weight loss, and so it is important that whilst purifying the system you avoid certain foods:

Helpful tips

It isn't only cutting out certain foods or including others that will help in your cellulite plan but equally important how you eat and how you prepare food:

• When choosing something to eat, consider its nutritional value and not only its taste
• Stick to regular mealtimes and try not to snack in between meals
• Eat slowly and chew your food thoroughly
• Do not drink liquids at mealtimes, as they tend to dilute the digestive juices therefore making it more difficult to digest food.
• Maintain an adequate water intake during the day.
• If eating fish, boil or bake it
• Avoid adding gravies, salad dressings and other rich sauces to your food. A healthier option is to mix a little oil with vinegar or lemon juice.
• Check on the label that the food is low fat

Planning Food

Whilst on the ban-the-cellulite programme, make sure that each day you try to eat:
✓ Three portions of vegetables
✓ Three portions of fruit
✓ Three portions of salad
✓ One portion of non-dairy yogurt, cheese or milk
✓ Two portions of nuts or fish
✓ One portion of brown rice

Drinking

Maintaining a healthy balance of fluids is always essential when cleansing out the system. Aim to drink at least 1.75 litres (3 pints) of water a day and if drinking plain water becomes a little boring, you can always add lemon, lime, honey or even ginger.

Fruit juices: these can be drunk in addition to the required amount of water, but if buying pre-packed check on the label that it is pure, unsweetened fruit juice and not the variety made up in water from fruit pulp. But better still, if you have a juicer you can make your own.

Herbal teas: there are lots of different varieties in supermarkets such as camomile, aniseed, dandelion, ginger and fennel.

Drinks to avoid:
• Alcohol   • Tea   • Coffee
• Fizzy drinks   • Hot chocolate

Dining out

A quick word about dining out whilst on the cellulite buster programme.

• Always have a glass or two of water before the meal to avoid eating too much and feeling bloated.

• If having a starter, choose vegetables and then if you are still peckish follow it up with a green salad.

• And just on the odd occasion you can have a special treat and choose a dessert.

• Try to stick with salads or vegetarian meals. Vegetable curries with rice are fine. Avoid naan bread because it contains raising agents and preservatives – remember you are trying to eat natural foods whenever possible.

Cellulite loves:
✗ Processed food
✗ Fizzy drinks
✗ Coffee
✗ Alcohol
✗ White bread

Cellulite hates:
✓ Lots of water
✓ Low fat foods
✓ Fresh fruit
✓ Fresh vegetables

Daily Treatments

To enable the programme to be successful there are certain things to follow each day, especially when detoxing the body.

Important foods and liquids

Hot lemon water: beginning the day with a hot cup of water and a squeeze of lemon or lime juice will freshen your mouth and give the liver a kick start – the largest organ involved in detoxing.

Water: cleansing, restoring and rejuvenating are the three basic principles in a detox programme and the one important thing which can help these three successfully is water. So make sure you drink plenty.

Liver tonic: the liver should be treated with kid gloves throughout the 28-day programme in order to do its job efficiently. To help do this, it needs a tonic in the form of at least two of the following foods each day:

- Two cups of fennel or dandelion tea
- A medium glass of pure carrot and beetroot juice
- A medium bunch of grapes
- Include a fresh clove of garlic in your food

Kidney tonics: as with the liver, the kidneys also have a hard job to do in detoxing and including certain foods in the diet will enable them to work more efficiently. Each day you must take two of the following:

- Sip a teaspoon of fresh honey dissolved in a cup of hot water
- A medium glass of cranberry juice
- Half a medium melon

Supplements: whenever changes in eating habits are made, they often affect the metabolic rate and if sufficient quantities of foods are not ingested, the body begins slowing down. At the beginning of your programme you may find it worthwhile to include certain supplements such as kelp, which equips the body with adequate amounts of iodine needed for balancing the metabolism and ideal to use when detoxing.

Vitamin supplements: it may be a good idea to include an all-round vitamin supplement in the initial stages of your detox programme to make sure the body is not being depleted of any essential nutrients. Generally, after two weeks, the body has adjusted and so you can stop taking them.

Whilst on the programme make sure each day you:

✓ Drink a cup of hot water and lemon/lime juice each morning
✓ Drink at least 1.75 litres (3 pints) of water during the day
✓ Take two liver tonics
✓ Take two kidney tonics
✓ Take a kelp supplement
✓ Take a multivitamin supplement for the first 15 days
✓ Eat three meals a day
✓ Eat one portion of rice (preferably short brown grain)
✓ Eat three portions of vegetables (one of which should be raw)
✓ Eat three portions of fruit
✓ Eat three portions of salad
✓ Eat one portion of non-dairy produce

Don't forget the outside

Just as you have dealt with the internal system cleansing and flushing out of poisonous toxins, you should begin to look outward and consider your overall wellbeing. The only way a programme can be termed a success is if both the outside and inside have been cleansed with a combination of exercise, relaxation and pampering.

Take a shower

Refreshing, invigorating and rejuvenating, an early morning shower is just what the body needs to jump-start it into action. But just as you are nearly finished, turn the cold tap on allowing the cold water to run over your body for one minute. It might sound a little barbaric but it will:

✔ tone up the skin
✔ tone up the muscles
✔ give the lymphatic system a jump start

Have a cold bath

This may sound a little harsh but in the second or third week try taking a cold bath. Experts advocate that they:

✔ ease menopausal side effects
✔ re-energize
✔ boost immunity
✔ reduce the risk of heart attack
✔ increase fertility

Simply run a cold bath, walk up and down in it to boost your circulation then take a deep breath and sit down waist deep for 3-5 minutes to cool the lower part of your body. Finally, for the brave hearted, submerge yourself up to your neck for 10-20 minutes, moving your limbs gently from time to time. Get out and briskly rub yourself dry. Wrap yourself in a snug blanket for at least 20 minutes to allow your body to recuperate. This is perhaps best done in the afternoon.

Each day throughout your cellulite-busting programme:

✔ Drink a glass of water each morning with a squeeze of lemon or lime juice added
✔ Take a cold shower/bath
✔ Do some dry skin brushing
✔ Take 30 minutes exercise
✔ Spend 5-10 minutes on acupressure
✔ Spend 5 minutes on quality breathing
✔ Take an Epsom salts bath every 5 days

Drink

Don't forget that early morning glass of water with an added squeeze of lemon or lime to kick start the body into action, cleanse your mouth and put a zing in your step.

Exercise

Exercises designed to tone and strengthen the abdominal area are recommended and form a very important part of the daily programme. As your stamina increases, gradually build up the number of repetitions you do. After the first week you may feel like taking up some outdoor exercises for a change.

Deep breathing

There is nothing quite so invigorating or relaxing as five minutes of deep, steady breathing to blow away those cobwebs. If you are wearing a skirt or trousers, undo the waistband so there is ample space for you to expand your stomach. Deep breathing is also excellent for helping to de-stress.

1. Sit in a quiet room.
2. Close your eyes and slowly breathe in, holding that breath to the count of five, then to the count of five slowly exhale through your mouth.
3. Repeat again several times.

Maintaining The Programme

Trying to change is never easy and there are bound to be occasions throughout the 28 days when you think why bother, what is the point of it all?

This programme isn't meant to be an ordeal – a little hard work perhaps, but not something you dread doing and so it is important to set aside an hour or so each day for some tender loving care.

Pamper yourself

You may well encounter negative days while on this programme which is why it is important always to have something to look forward to. If you feel low, spend a day with friends, treat yourself to something, visit the hairdresser or listen to your favourite music.

Exfoliate

In order to clear the skin of dead skin cells and freshen it up, a regular facial scrub does it the world of good. Don't just use a facial scrub over the face; remember the elbows and knees also benefit from this beauty treatment. Rinse thoroughly with tepid water.

Quick oatmeal scrub: Make up a paste of oatmeal and water, then apply it to the face. Once it has dried and the skin feels tight, rub it off using your fingers to clean away all the dead skin cells. Rinse thoroughly with tepid water.

Wheatgerm exfoliator: This is ideal for all skin types. Mix together 1 tablespoon of wheatgerm with 1 tablespoon of single cream in a bowl until they form a paste. Massage it gently over the skin, and then rinse clear with tepid water.

Epsom salts bath

Speed up the elimination of toxins from the skin and improve its circulation with an Epsom salts bath. Run the bath water and add 225-450g ($1/2$-1lb) of Epsom salts. Soak for about 20 minutes, and when you get

out, keep yourself warm by piling on lots of clothes – this will help the body to continue sweating out the toxins. Most chemists and health food stores sell Epsom salts.

Olive oil treatment

Can't afford a trip to the hairdresser but your hair feels in need of some attention? Try an olive oil treatment. Put some olive oil into a bowl and warm it gently over a saucepan of water. When it is warm but not too hot, apply it over the hair and massage well into the scalp. Leave it on for 15 minutes, then shampoo thoroughly.

Scream

Do you often feel like having a good scream, shouting and yelling like a banshee until all that pent-up emotion and frustration inside has been expelled? So what are you waiting for? Go for it! Just make sure you don't frighten anyone else with your actions. You'll feel so much better afterwards. Another equally good method for 'letting it all out' is to punch some pillows!

Acupressure techniques

When you feel completely stressed and worn out, you may well benefit from a little acupressure, a common term for a technique that uses pressure in order to arouse certain energy points throughout the body. In doing so, it corrects any imbalance, moves any energy blockages and helps treat specific aliments. It was first discovered by the Chinese over 5,000 years ago and is something that you can do in your own home.

Practise it up to five times a day. Do not practise it if you are pregnant or have a medical condition.

To help ease exhaustion: Using the thumb and forefinger of one hand, apply pressure on the point in the middle of your little finger on the other hand, just

below the top bone. Hold for 20 seconds before slowly releasing and repeat again four times, waiting 10 seconds between applying the pressure.

Balneotherapy

Have you ever tried balneotherapy? It is so relaxing if practised once a week and involves immersing yourself in a bath at a temperature of just below 32°C for 20 minutes. Add some seaweed powder (available at health food shops) and you will find it lowers your blood pressure, boosts metabolism and aids elimination of toxins from the body.

Days 1–7

You've done all the preparatory work and so can look forward to the following 28-day programme. By the end of it you should feel invigorated and rejuvenated.

Whether you are a working woman or a busy mum, the next 28 days will include some big changes in your life, so be prepared. Make up a chart (see page 31) and stick it on your kitchen wall so that you will remember what you must include each day in your programme.

Don't forget to keep a diary to record your everyday thoughts. Even if you have had a rotten day, write it down and then try to understand why it was such a bad day.

Here is a typical plan for day one, but naturally times will differ and the order in which activities are done may also change according to your individual lifestyle and work commitments.

7.15am Wake up and have a glass of water with a squeeze of lemon juice.
8.00am Get the circulation moving and give your body a dry skin brush. Then jump into the shower –

don't forget to turn on a blast of cold water before you come out.
8.45am Breakfast – on the first day opt for some fresh fruit such as papaya or pineapple and eat it slowly. Complement it with a cup of herbal tea.
9.15am Start the day the way you mean to end and do some power walking.
11.00am Time for relaxation and quality breathing. Have a glass of water afterwards and sit down to listen to some music.
1.00pm Time for lunch. Try a salad today with a lemon dressing. Finish off with a piece of fruit.
2.15pm Why not try an exercise routine for the stomach area.
4.00pm Time for some pampering and recuperation after the exercising, so make some of your own lip balm – it's so easy to do (see recipe).
6.00pm Prepare dinner.
7.00pm De-stressing. It's been a hard day and you have made many changes, so sit in a quiet room and do some acupressure.
8.00pm Have an aromatherapy bath. Put some candles around the room, add some of your favourite essential oils, then relax. Then have an early night.

Don't forget – as you complete each activity, tick it off on your chart and before you go to sleep remember to record in your diary how you felt, both the good and bad points. Then write down what you intend doing the following day, or prepare the food you intend eating.

Remainder of the week

The first week of anything new is always the hardest, so be kind to yourself. Making changes is never easy so do them gradually. Instead of going out, stay in and do a workout programme. Spend one morning cooking a batch of meals to pop into the freezer so you won't have to worry about what you are going to eat. You won't notice many changes in the first week so don't be too impatient.

Strawberry lip balm
A simple lip balm that is easy to make. You can replace the strawberry essential oil with any other, if you wish.
2 tablespoons petroleum jelly
1 teaspoon beeswax
12 drops strawberry essential oil

Melt the petroleum jelly and beeswax in a small bowl over a pan of boiling water. Add the strawberry essential oil, stir well. Transfer into a small container and leave to set.

Measurements chart

As you change your routine and reform your eating habits, you will find that you are not only banishing cellulite but looking good and feeling better. You will have toned up muscles all over your body to give you a slimmer look and lots more energy!

You can record your measurements each week using this simple chart.

	Week 1	Week 2	Week 3	Week 4
Date				
Weight				
Bust				
Waist				
Hips				
Thighs				

Days 8–14

With the first week over, certain routines should be established, but remember no slacking and no adding in foods that are banned!

7.15am Have a glass of water with a squeeze of lime juice

8.00am Get the circulation moving and give your body a dry skin brush. Then massage the skin before having a shower.

8.45am Breakfast. During this week you can have something more substantial for breakfast. So how about porridge made with water instead of milk.

10.15am Do the full exercise routine this morning. Repeat each of the hip, thigh and stomach exercises from pages 8–11 ten times. This should take at least 30 minutes – don't rush it and work at your own speed.

11.15am Time for relaxation and quality breathing. Have a glass of water afterwards and sit down to listen to some music.

1.00pm Time for lunch. Always finish off with a piece of fruit.

2.15pm Be a total water baby today and go along to your local swimming pool for an hour. If 20 minutes' swimming burns up 180 calories, just imagine what an hour's worth will use up.

4.00pm You've had a busy day so you will need some relaxation. Why not give yourself a facial and see how relaxed you feel afterwards. See face mask recipe.

6.00pm Prepare dinner. Tonight have a salad with lots of fresh vegetables and some fruit.

7.00pm Another tiring day, so why not have a cold

bath to wake your system up.

9.00pm Remember that comedy video you bought and haven't had a chance to watch, well there is no time like the present and you will feel so totally relaxed that when it has finished you will be ready for bed.

Don't forget - as you do each activity, tick it off on your chart and before you go to sleep remember to record in your diary how you felt, the good and bad points.

Remainder of the week

Add in different exercises or borrow a yoga video from the library and begin studying it. Try out some different recipes using the foods that you are allowed. And remember to keep kneading at that cellulite.

Honey and grape face mask

Take a handful of grapes, 1 tablespoon honey, 1 egg yolk and 1 teaspoon olive oil. De-seed and skin the grapes. Pop all the ingredients into a liquidizer. When blended thoroughly, apply to the face. Leave for 15 minutes, then rinse off with warm water. The honey moisturizes the skin while the egg yolk provides it with protein and the olive oil softens it.

Days 15–21

It's the third week and by now you should start to see some slight changes. You will feel healthier and more energetic and you may well notice some changes in your skin.

7.15am Wake up and have a glass of water with a squeeze of lemon juice. Give your body a well-deserved stretch and feel totally invigorated. Lying in bed for 8 hours can cause muscular aches and pains to develop and this inactivity can ultimately lead to a build-up of lactic acid in the muscles, resulting in pain and stiffness. That is why the daily routine of stretching the arms and body is invaluable.

8.00am Get the circulation moving and give yourself a dry skin brush. Then jump into the shower.

8.45am Breakfast.

10.15am Today clean the house from top to bottom. The added incentive is that the harder you do each individual task, the more calories the body burns!

11.15am Time for some breathing exercises and follow up with a cup of herbal tea.

1.00pm Time for lunch. How about a healthy, nutritious and tasty jacket potato today?.

2.15pm Go to the shops and do some simple exercises when standing in the queues. Clench your buttocks, hold for a few seconds and then release.

4.00pm Back at home do some hip and thigh exercises before sitting down with a cup of herbal tea.

6.00pm Prepare dinner. Tonight, perhaps a salad.

7.00pm Do some meditation in a quiet room.

9.00pm Have a detox bath and then another early night.

Don't forget – as you do each activity, tick it off on your chart and before you go to sleep remember to record in your diary how you felt, both the good and bad points.

Remainder of the week

You are nearly at the end of the programme and by now you will probably be looking and feeling a whole lot better but don't start slacking. It is often towards the end when most people do stop, but unless you complete the programme you can't expect to reach your target of banishing the cellulite.

Days 22–28

This is nearly it, the end of your 28-day programme and you have survived. You should begin to feel more energetic now, largely due to a healthier diet combined with regular exercise and relaxation. So don't give up now.

7.15am Wake up and have a glass of water with a squeeze of lime juice. Get the circulation moving and give your body a dry skin brush. Then jump into the shower.

8.00am Breakfast.

8.45am Do the full exercise programme.

10.15am Have a cup of herbal tea and then sit down and relax by watching the TV or listening to some favourite music.

11.15am Get ready to meet some friends in town. Spend time putting on your make-up and choose clothes that will show off your new look.

1.00pm Time for lunch. Choose something healthy and have a glass of fresh orange juice.

2.15pm Back at home, take a cold bath and practise balneotherapy.

4.00pm Do some acupressure.

6.00pm To celebrate the end of the programme why not go out for a meal, but remember to choose your meal wisely. You are allowed one glass of wine.

9.00pm Sit down and put your feet up – you deserve it.

Don't forget – as you do each activity, tick it off on your chart and before you go to sleep remember to record in your diary how you felt, both the good and bad points.

Remainder of the week

Keep up with the routine, even to the very last day. On the final day why not celebrate and treat yourself to some new exercise clothes because from now on, as you feel so much better, exercise will become part of your daily life.

Activity Record Chart

Record your activities every day using this table

DAILY ACTIVITIES	1	2	3	4	5	6	7	8	9	10	11	12	13	14	15	16	17	18	19	20	21	22	23	24	25	26	27	28
Glass of hot water and lemon or lime juice																												
Dry skin brushing																												
Cold water bath/shower																												
Breakfast																												
Lunch																												
Dinner																												
2 liver tonics																												
2 kidney tonics																												
1 kelp supplement																												
Multivitamin supplement (15 days)																												
1.75 litres (3 pints) water																												
1 portion short brown rice																												
3 portions vegetables (1 raw)																												
3 portions fresh fruit																												
3 portions salad																												
1 portion non-dairy food																												
30 mins exercise																												
5–10 mins acupressure																												
5 mins quality breathing																												
Epsom salts bath every five days																												

Congratulations!

It was probably the hardest 28 days of your life but you have succeeded – you have banished the cellulite and proved it can be done.

It might not have been plain sailing, you may have well faltered along the way and succumbed to the occasional bar of chocolate, but that doesn't really matter provided you got back on to the programme immediately!

And just think of all the money you have saved by not going along to a beauty salon for hours of expensive treatment. It will probably be enough to allow you to treat yourself to a new bathing costume to show off those smooth long legs this summer.

But now that you have come this far, you don't want to risk dropping the routine and allowing the cellulite return. So be sensible, and add some of the changes you have adopted throughout the programme into your daily life.

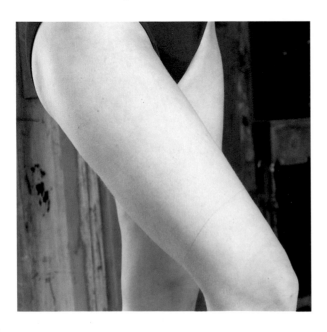

Things to continue after the programme
- Exercise
- Following a healthy diet
- Make sure that you drink at least 1.75 litres (3 pints) of water a day
- Don't forget body brushing when you have a bath or shower
- And, above all, be proud of the way you look